746·664 00788336

You may renew this item for a further period if it is not required by another user.

MALVERN HILLS COLLEGE

part of **WCG**

LIBRARY

Albert Rd North Malvern WR142YH

NORMAL LOAN (3 WEEKS)

For enqquiries and reservations tel ;

(016845984594

or Text: 07747 390008

Simply Shibori

Handmade, hand-dyed projects for the home

FIONA FAGAN

NEW HOLLAND

To Mark, Ella and Tessa

CONTENTS

INTRODUCTION

ABOUT SHIBORI

Over 1,000 years old, the modern Shibori methods we use today stay close to their traditional roots when the technique first entered Japan from China during the 8th century. The term shibori derives from the word shiboru meaning "to wring, squeeze, and press". It is a range of techniques that involve manipulating, folding, twisting, compressing, stitching, and binding the cloth before dyeing in order to create distinctive resist, geometric and floral patterns. Therefore the technique used in combination with the type of fabric will give very different and varied results. Techniques can also be combined to create more elaborate designs.

During the past few decades, artisans and designers from around the world have been reinterpreting the traditional Japanese Shibori processes and patterns into modern fashion design, expanding the choice of materials, the size of design elements, and the finishing process from traditional dyeing, creating modern, creatively dyed commercial, consumer products.

SHIBORI TECHNIQUES

Arashi – (Japanese word for Storm) Pole wrapping. The fabric is wrapped on a diagonal around the pole, and then tightly bound with string. The cloth is scrunched or pushed down to one end of the pole creating small diagonal pleated patterns, which suggest the torrid rain of a heavy storm. Thin, fine fabrics, such as silk or cotton voile, will give the best results for this technique.

Itajima – The use of shapes to resist the dye. The materials used as the shapes were traditionally wooden but today you can use Perspex or plastic, which are clamped with fabric between the shapes to resist the dye.

Nui – Stitched. A simple running stitch, which is pulled to gather up the fabric. The threads must be pulled tightly to resist the dye and the threads should be knotted to hold tight. This is a time-consuming technique but you can create very detailed designs and patterns.

Kumo – ("Spider web" Shibori) Pleating and bound resist. This technique is created by pleating sections of cloth very finely and evenly. The cloth is then bound in close sections resulting in a spiderweb-like design.

FABRICS USED FOR SHIBORI

Linen – Linen's qualities include strength for durability, ability to withstand abrasion and amazing absorption properties, which makes it a perfect choice for Shibori.

Cotton – Comes in very fine, crisp organdy through to a heavy, robust canvas, which will give a very different result when dyed with indigo.

Silk – Will give you luminosity, lustre and will produce a vibrant color, feeling soft to the touch.

Wool – Absorbs dye with depth, uniformity and permanently. You may need to pre-wash your wool to remove any additive or lanoline, which will resist the dye's absorption.

INDIGO DYE RECIPE

Indigo is a dark blue crystalline powder. The natural dye comes from several species of plants, but most natural indigo is obtained from plants in the genus *Indigofera,* which are native to the tropics. Nearly all indigo produced today is synthetic. It is most commonly used in the production of denim cloth for blue jeans.

Indigo is not soluble in water, so for it to be dissolved, it must undergo a chemical change. When a submerged fabric is removed from the dye vat, the indigo changes from green to blue which is the oxidization of the indigo, hence the oxygen in the air reverts the indigo to its insoluble form.

Most natural fibers such as silk, linen, cotton or wool absorb indigo dye. The fabrics should be soaked, de-greased or scoured before dyeing to remove any barrier (grease, sericin, or starch) so the dye can penetrate the fiber evenly.

To make your vat you will need:

- 240 g (8½ oz) soda ash
- 50 g (2 oz) indigo crystals
- 160 g (5½ oz) sodium hydrosulphite
- 10–14 litres (338–473 fl oz) warm water in a large tub
- 500 ml (17 fl oz) boiling water in a plastic jug
- Face mask, if indoors

Mixing the vat:

- Dissolve the soda ash into the plastic jug with 50 ml (2 fl oz) boiling water.
- Pour your soda/boiling water into the large tub.
- Sprinkle the indigo crystals into your tub of warm water.
- Sprinkle sodium hydrosulphite into tub.
- Stir gently so as not to introduce oxygen to the vat. Cover with a lid and wrap in towels to keep warm.

Prepare your fabric

Before you dye your fabric you will have to prepare it by washing it in a little detergent to remove any grease or starch. This makes it easier for the dye to bond to the fibers.

Ready to dye

- Wear gloves when you are dyeing with indigo.
- Submerge your prepared fabric in the vat for 10–15 minutes.
- Remove the fabric from the vat and watch it change color from green to blue, which is the chemical process of oxidization.
- Rinse the fabric in cold water with a cup of salt in the water to fix the color. Rinse until the water runs clear.
- Enjoy your shibori creations.
- Don't forget to rinse the clamps, marbles, etc., ready for the next time you want to shibori.

Note: Keep a small amount of the chemicals to revitalize your vat. If your vat turns blue instead of yellowy green add sodium hydrosulphite. If white specks appear in your vat, add 1 teaspoon of caustic soda. Use dishwashing liquid to wash your fabric to avoid stripping the color off.

Happy Dyeing!

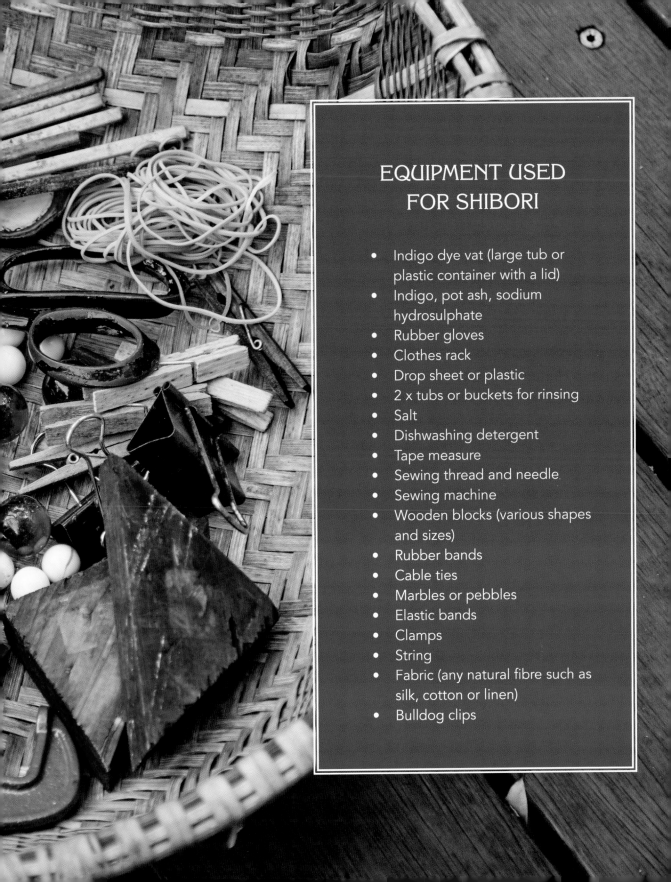

EQUIPMENT USED FOR SHIBORI

- Indigo dye vat (large tub or plastic container with a lid)
- Indigo, pot ash, sodium hydrosulphate
- Rubber gloves
- Clothes rack
- Drop sheet or plastic
- 2 x tubs or buckets for rinsing
- Salt
- Dishwashing detergent
- Tape measure
- Sewing thread and needle.
- Sewing machine
- Wooden blocks (various shapes and sizes)
- Rubber bands
- Cable ties
- Marbles or pebbles
- Elastic bands
- Clamps
- String
- Fabric (any natural fibre such as silk, cotton or linen)
- Bulldog clips

Dyeing Tips

The wonderful thing about shibori is you can practice with the techniques. After experimenting, you will have produced lots of samples to determine which designs you like best. I cut 40 x 40 cm (15¾ x 15¾ in) squares of cotton fabric to practice the different shibori methods. It is also a great idea (a suggestion from one of my students) to photograph your method because it is often hard to remember a technique…which can be frustrating if you really like it!

PICK YOUR PROJECT

Choose your fabric, making sure it is appropriate for the finished application.

Gather your materials to make patterns before you start. Many of the materials used for shibori are things you probably already have around the house — wooden blocks, rubber bands, jar lids, cable ties and marbles.

Wait for a sunny day, if possible, so you can do the dyeing outside!

DON'T RUSH

Take your time preparing the fabric, dyeing, soaking, rinsing, and unfolding your project. The finished product will take time. Instead of trying to do everything in one day (binding the fabric, soaking the fabric, dyeing the fabric, washing the fabric, drying the fabric, and cleaning up the mess), I try to break up my tasks and work slow and steady. The most important part of shibori is the binding of your material. If you rush this part of the process, you'll regret the end results. You shouldn't hurry the untying or unfolding of the shibori fabric too soon as it can result in patterns with less contrast and may cause a crisp design to blur. This is also important with rinsing the dye thoroughly (until the water runs clear) while the fabric is still bound.

YOU WILL MAKE A MESS

So be prepared! Indigo will get on anything and everything, so be careful about where you're working. Use buckets, drop clothes and old rags. I love hanging my dyed creations on my clothes line and watch them develop in color as they oxidize. Lower your stress levels and enjoy the process, it is addictive. Plus, working outside will reduce your cleaning time after you've spent a whole day stooped over your vat.

Make sure your cloth runs clear after dyeing. Use a little dishwashing liquid to wash your fabric to avoid stripping the color off after you have finished dyeing it.

MAINTAINING YOUR VAT

- When placing your prepared fabric into the vat, make sure you have minimum disruption of the surface flower (shiny skin on the surface of the vat) to minimise the oxidization of the dye vat.
- When removing your dyed shibori, try not to let the dye drip back into the vat as this will also oxidize the vat, rendering it unusable. I use a small container to catch the drips as I'm removing the item from the vat.
- Keep a small amount of the chemicals to revitalize your vat. If your vat turns blue instead of yellowy green, add Sodium Hydrosulphite. If white specks appear in your vat, add 1 teaspoon of caustic soda.

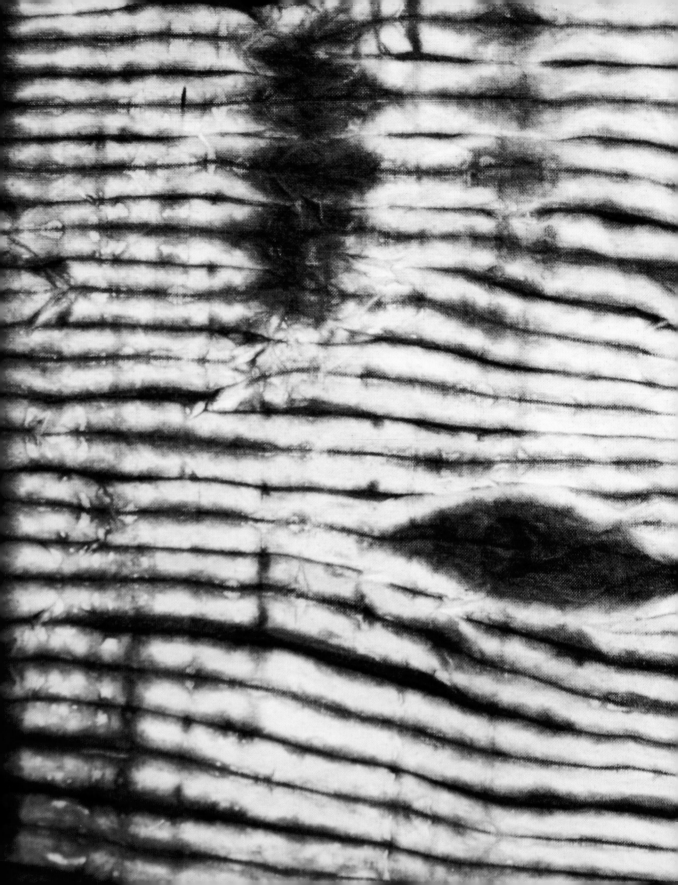

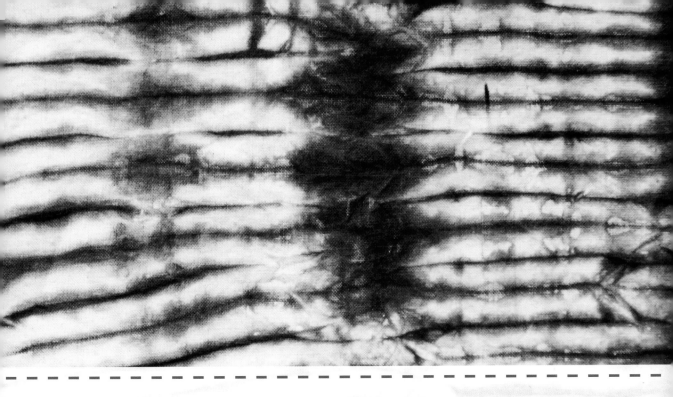

PROJECTS

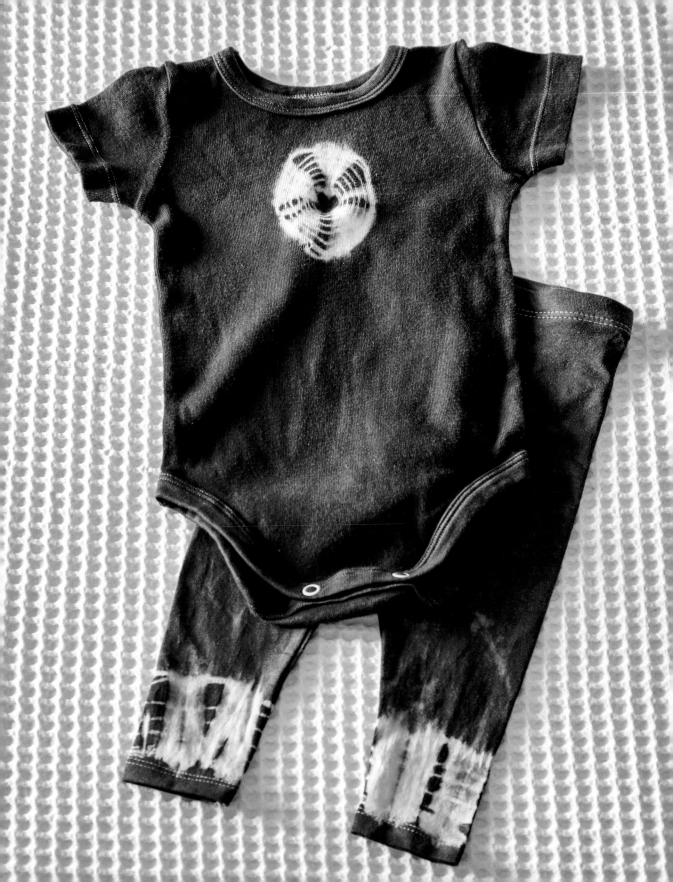

Baby's Bodysuit and Leggings

A great way to turn a rather boring bodysuit and leggings into something individual and creative for that special little person!

This is such a simple and quick technique which will give you a great result.

YOU WILL NEED:
- 100 per cent white cotton bodysuit (for a 3–6 month old)
- Cotton/elastene leggings (for a 3–6 month old)
- String
- Scissors
- Dye vat (see page 13)
- Rubber gloves
- Drop sheet
- Drying rack

Note: I have tested the elastane/cotton and it will absorb the dye but may need to be submerged in the vat for a little longer than the bodysuit to get the same strength of color (if that is what you're after!).

SHIBORI TECHNIQUE:
Bodysuit:
1. Find the center front of the bodysuit and pinch the fabric so you can tie a slipknot around the fabric. Pull the slipknot tight.
2. Start to wind the string as tightly as you can around the pinched fabric, making sure you leave an even gap between each wind, to get an even amount of fabric exposed to the dye.
3. Keep winding for approximately 5 cm (2 in) and tie off with a firm knot. If you are using a larger bodysuit, your tied area can be larger so the design is in proportion with the whole garment.

Leggings:
1. Make very small concertina pleats in each lower leg of the leggings and then hold both legs together to wind both legs together. This will make your pattern the same for each leg.
2. Tie a slipknot at one end of your string and loop it around both legs, holding them together.
3. Wind the string evenly up the legs tightly. Continue to wind for approximately 5 cm (2 in). If your leggings are a larger size, you may want to continue winding up the leg to create a larger pattern.
4. Tie off your string tightly at the desired length.
5. Now you are ready to place your

garments into the vat. If you want a light blue finish only, leave your bodysuit in for 30 seconds. If you want more intense color, leave it in for 1–5 minutes.

6. Massage the garments in the vat to maximize the dye absorbency.
7. Remove carefully from the vat, trying not to drip indigo back into the vat. This will create oxidization, therefore reducing the life of the vat.
8. Squeeze or press the excess dye from the garments using an old towel.
9. Rinse in water with 1 tablespoon of salt to set the color. Rinse until no dye comes out of the fabric.
10. Hang on the rack to dry.

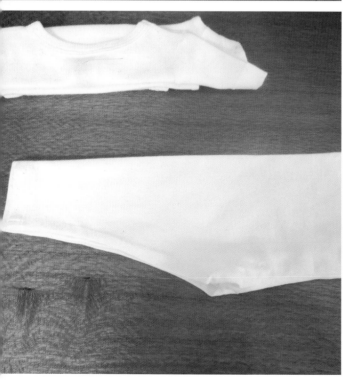

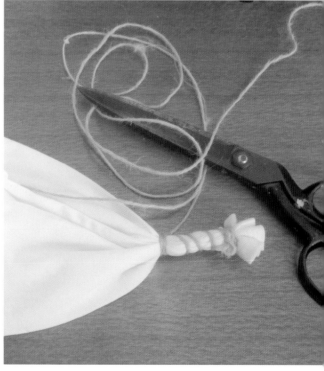

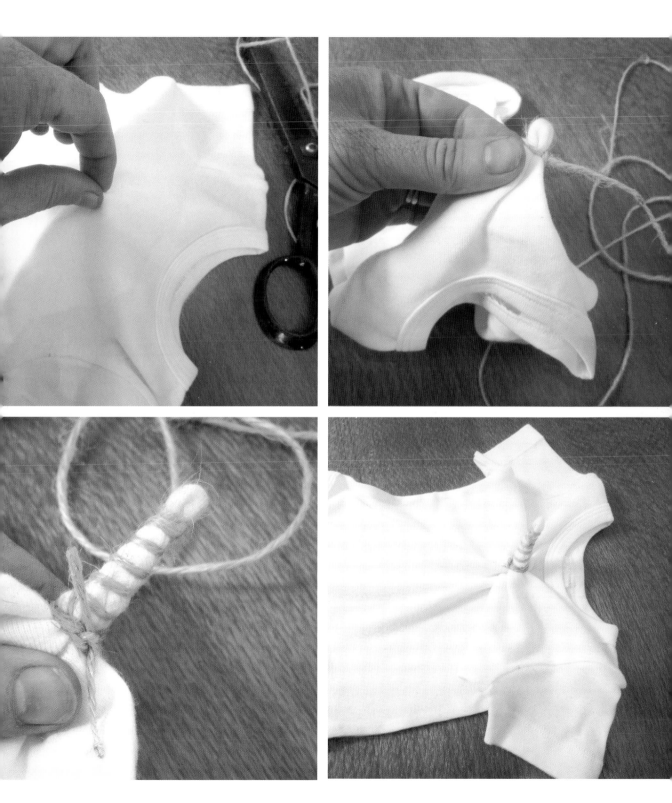

Beach Sarong

A great accessory for the beach or pool. Cotton voile is lightweight and cool to wear, as well as quick-drying if it gets wet. It takes takes up very little room in your bag, for that holiday or weekend away!

YOU WILL NEED:

- White cotton voile or lawn 120 x 210 cm (47 x 82½ in). Finished dimensions will be approximately 115 x 205 cm (45 x 80½ in). (This may vary depending on the person's body shape and if you want a full width sarong or a half width. If you have a favorite sarong, measure it to use as a guide.)
- 2 x wooden triangles
- Large clamps
- Dye vat (see page 13)
- Rubber gloves
- 2 x tubs of water, one with detergent (1 tablespoon to clean) and one with salt (1 tablespoon to fix the color)
- Drop sheet
- Drying rack

TO MAKE THE SARONG:

1. Cut the fabric to 120 x 210 cm (47 x 82½ in), this will give you a seam allowance of 2.5 cm (1 in) on each edge.
2. Fold your edge 1.25 cm (½ in) and press with an iron. Turn again 1.25 cm (½ in) and stitch, using white sewing thread, on your sewing machine. Make sure your corners are neatly turned and pressed before sewing.
3. Finish each side with a couple of reverse stiches to reinforce.
4. Now your sarong is ready to prepare your shibori design before dyeing in the vat. I have chosen to use the Itajime technique for my design.

SHIBORI TECHNIQUE:

1. Fold the sarong in half lengthways so it is long and narrow.
2. Start at one end and fold into a concertina fold approximately 12–13 cm (4¾–5 in) wide folds.
3. Fold into four folds and place wooden triangle shapes on each side and clamp with "G" clamps (see tools).
4. Place clamped fabric into warm water that has a drop of dishwashing detergent to remove any fabric stiffener. This will help to maximize the even absorption of the dye.
5. Prepare your vat for dyeing.
6. Place the clamped fabric into the vat with minimum disruption of the surface flower (shiny skin on the surface of the vat) to minimize the oxidization of the dye vat.
7. Leave in the vat for the about

10 minutes (but if you want the color to be more intense leave it in for a longer period of time).

8. Massage the folds in your fabric to get the maximum dye absorption.

9. Remove from the vat and press excess dye out of the fabric using an old towel. Remove the clamps and shapes and unfold gently.

10. Watch your fabric turn from green to blue as the indigo dye oxidizes.

11. Plunge dyed fabric into a bucket of water to remove any excess dye. Continue until the water runs clear.

12. Hang on the line and watch the colors develop.

13. For colorfastness, rinse your fabric in a solution of water with some vinegar or salt added to hold the color.

Belt

A quick and easy project to create an original belt to wear with your favorite denim jeans or skirt. I have used D rings because you can adjust the belt to fit different waist measurements, which helps if you are making this as a gift for someone.

YOU WILL NEED:

- Shibori dyed fabric (Cotton canvas would be the ideal fabric) – 130 x 20 cm (51 x 8 in)
- Interfacing (medium to heavyweight)
- Tape measure
- Fabric scissors
- Pins
- Sewing machine
- Thread and sewing needle
- D Ring Belt loops (from a craft or haberdashery store)
- Dye vat (see page 13)
- Rubber gloves
- 2 x tubs of water, one with detergent (1 tablespoon to clean) and one with salt (1 tablespoon to fix the color)
- Drop sheet
- Drying rack

SHIBORI TECHNIQUE:

1. You will need to have the belt measurement to prepare your fabric.
2. Use your sewing needle and a contrast color thread to stitch a simple running stitch in three lines for the whole length of the fabric.
3. Start by making a knot at one end of your thread.
4. Make your stitches about 5 mm (¼ in) long. Iron three folds in your fabric to help guide you when you are stitching. Alternatively, you could use a chalk line to follow which will later disappear when you dye your fabric.
5. When you have completed all three rows, you can gather all three threads and draw them up so the fabric is gathered. Gather them as tightly as you can because this will be where your dye will be resisted. To keep them tightly gathered, knot the threads or wind them around the gathered fabric.
6. Now it's ready to put in a tub of warm water with a teaspoon of detergent, massage. This will help the indigo dye to be absorbed evenly throughout the fabric. Squeeze out excess liquid.
7. Place in the vat for 2–5 minutes depending on the depth of color you are after.
8. Remove and squeeze out any excess dye using an old towel to absorb the excess.
9. Cut the stitching and undo the gathering to reveal your design.
10. Watch the green color oxidize and turn blue.

11. Wash in water with a tablespoon of salt to help fix the color.

12. Rinse until the water runs clear, then hang out to dry.

TO MAKE UP THE BELT:

1. Measure the circumference of where you will be wearing the belt, either on the waist, hips or somewhere in the middle.

2. Add about 15 cm (6 in) to the length, this will include the hem allowance, the casing to attach the belt buckles, and the extra on the end, which hangs from the belt buckle.

3. Cut 2 lengths of fabric either both in shibori or you could use a contrast fabric so you can reverse your belt to get a different look. The width of your strips should be 2 cm (¾ in) wider than the inside width of your belt loop/buckle, this will allow for seam allowances of 1 cm (½ in).

4. Cut 1 length of interfacing the same dimensions as the outer fabric.

5. Put the outer fabrics right sides together, laying the interfacing on top and pin all three layers together.

6. Stitch together the strips, removing the pins as you go using 1 cm (½ in) seam allowance. Check to make sure the seams are the correct width to fit the belt loops.

7. Trim back the excess fabric.

8. Turn your belt out by using a safety pin at one end of the opening and thread it through the fabric tube until it comes out the other end.

9. Press.

10. Thread both of your D rings onto the belt fabric, fold the belt fabric 5 cm (2 in) at one end, encasing the D ring, press, then fold again 1.5 cm (½ in). Stitch along folded edge to create a loop to hold the D rings. Make sure you reverse stitch at the beginning and the end so it doesn't come undone.

11. Fold in 5 mm (¼ in) of the other end of your belt inside the opening, press and slipstitch or machine stitch to close, finishing the end of the belt neatly.

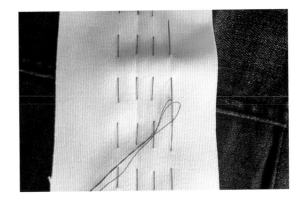

Bed Throw

I'm going to cheat with this project and go buy myself a 100 per cent cotton bed throw. It has a woven pattern through it, which will give an added design element. Think big and bold with this project, as it is bulky.

YOU WILL NEED:
- 100 per cent cotton bed throw — 150 x 250 cm (59 x 98 in)
- 2 x circular lids (I used old melamine plates as they are strong and ridged, holding their shape when clamped)
- Clamps (heavy-duty)
- Dye vat (see page 13)
- Rubber gloves
- 2 x tubs of water, one with detergent (1 tablespoon to clean) and one with salt (1 tablespoon to fix the color)
- Drop sheet
- Drying rack

SHIBORI TECHNIQUE:
1. Fold the bed throw in half.
2. Work out the width of your folds depending on the width of your plates.
3. My plates have a diameter of 21 cm (8¼ in) so my folds will be 28–30 cm (11–12 in) so the plate sits in the middle of the folded fabric.
4. Concertina your fabric until it is all folded. It will look like a long tube.
5. Now fold your fabric tube in half and concertina fold it so it looks like a square. It should be big enough to clamp the plates in the middle without overlapping the folded edges.
6. Clamp with your heavy-duty clamps on both sides of your fabric.
7. Now it's ready to put in a tub of warm water with 1 teaspoon of detergent. Massage. This will help the indigo dye to be absorbed evenly throughout the fabric.
8. Place in the vat for 2–5 minutes, depending on the depth of color you are after.
9. Remove and squeeze out any excess dye using an old towel to absorb the excess.
10. Remove the clamps and circular lids and unfold to reveal your design.
11. Watch the green color oxidize and turn blue.
12. Wash in water with 1 tablespoon of salt to help fix the color.
13. Rinse really well until the water runs clear. This is very important because you will be putting your throw on other bed linen, which may be white and you don't want color to transfer to your other linen.
14. Hang on the line to dry.
15. Double-check that the color is fast. If not, rinse again in salted water.

Brooch

A simple and inexpensive accessory, which can be worn on a hat, badge or brooch.

YOU WILL NEED:
- White silk or cotton fabric — 50 x 50 cm (19½ x 19½ in)
- Large 64 mm (2½ in) self-cover button
- Brooch pin/clasp
- Marbles
- Elastic bands
- Dye vat (see page 13)
- Rubber gloves
- 2 x tubs of water, one with detergent (1 tablespoon to clean) and one with salt (1 tablespoon to fix the color)
- Drop sheet
- Drying rack
- Embroidery threads
- Sewing needle
- Hot glue gun
- Glue

SHIBORI TECHNIQUE:
1. Place your fabric over a marble and hold in place by wrapping a rubber band around the fabric containing the marble.
2. You can repeat this on your fabric and then use the leftover fabric for other small projects, like making cards.
3. Now you are ready to put in a tub of warm water with 1 teaspoon of detergent. Massage. This will help the indigo dye to be absorbed evenly throughout the fabric. Squeeze out excess liquid.
4. Place in the vat for 2–5 minutes depending on the depth of color you are after.
5. Remove and squeeze out any excess dye using an old towel.
6. Cut the rubber bands and remove marbles. Unfold to reveal your design. Watch the green color oxidize and turn blue.
7. Wash in water with 1 tablespoon of salt to help fix the color.
8. Rinse the fabric pieces until the water runs clear and then hang them out to dry. Now you can embroider your fabric with French knots.

Notes: I have used a fine cotton for this project — thick enough so you don't have to use double layers of fabric to conceal the button base.

Select your shibori design by wrapping it around the button to make sure the design is the right proportion for the button.

HOW TO MAKE FRENCH KNOTS:

1. Thread your embroidery thread and find the center of your shibori motif to start your French knot detail. Start by putting a knot in the end of your thread. You will need both hands. With your non-needle hand pinch the thread a few inches from where it exits the fabric. Hold it taut with your hand not holding the needle (that's important).

2. Place your needle in front of this stretch of thread. Notice the needle is in front of the thread, not coming from behind it. This will make the next step easier, and will prevent the knot from going all wonky later on.

3. Wind the thread around the needle once or twice, depending on if you want a bigger or smaller knot. Continue the tension of the thread with your left hand (non-needle hand) to prevent it from uncoiling.
   IMPORTANT: Keep your hand holding the needle still while winding it with the thread in this step.

4. You've wound the thread around the needle, the coil is pulled nice and taut. Next, (this is an important one) re-insert the tip of your needle just next to, but not into the same exit point on your fabric. If you enter the same hole, your knot may pop all the way through and disappear when you finish. Simply return at a point a little bit away from the exit point and hold it right there! Keep your needle in this position.

Don't push it all the way through just yet.

5. Give the thread a little downward tug with that hand, so that the coil will tighten up, and slide down your needle to make a little bundle against the surface of your fabric.

6. With your coil snugly held in position against the surface, push your needle all the way through the fabric.

7. You've just pulled your needle, and the thread trailing behind it, down through the center of the coil that was wrapped around the needle.

8. Voilà! A French knot! Now continue using French knots to create a center using various colors which will give the shibori texture.

TO MAKE UP THE BROOCH:

1. Cut out a 7.5 cm (3 in) diameter circle of your shibori dyed fabric with your French knot in the center. If the fabric you use is sheer, cut an extra layer of fabric or interfacing.

2. Center button top over the fabric, working the fabric onto the button teeth. Continue working around the button, stretching the fabric for a tight, smooth fit.

3. Snap back plate on button.

4. If your fabric is thick, use a thread spool to help snap on the back plate.

5. Use your hot glue gun to attach your brooch pin on the back of the button.

6. You can either place in the center

or towards the top of the brooch depending on the final use. Center for attaching to a hat, or towards the top if you are wearing on a garment (so it doesn't drop forward or flop down showing the back of the brooch).

7. Enjoy!

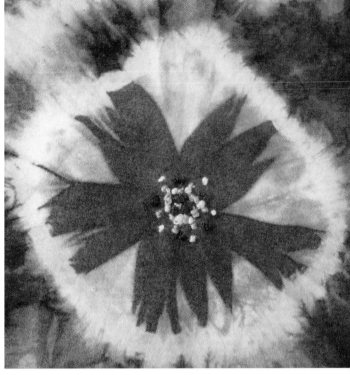

Patched Cushion Cover

If you have done some experimentation with shibori this is a great way to use those small pieces of samples to create a lovely keepsake showing all the different techniques used.

YOU WILL NEED:

- 2 x Shibori fabric samples 53 x 28 cm (21 x 11 in)
- Backing fabric (plain or shibori) 53 x 53 cm (21 x 21 in)
- Cable ties, string
- Wooden blocks
- Zipper 30 cm (12 in)
- Sewing machine
- Thread
- Tape measure
- Scissors
- Pins
- Dye vat (see page 13)
- Rubber gloves
- 2 x tubs of water, one with detergent (1 tablespoon to clean) and one with salt (1 tablespoon to fix the color)
- Drop sheet
- Drying rack
- Cushion inner 50 x 50 cm (19½ x 19½ in)

PREPARING YOUR SHIBORI FABRIC:

Fabric 1: Circles

1. Pinch your fabric and tie with some string using a slip knot.
2. Continue to wind the string around the fabric until you have the desired diameter of your circle, approximately 10 cm (4 in), then tie off using another slip knot.
3. For the small circle, repeat the method above only looping the string once and fastening it to create a circle design. Tie using another slip knot.
4. Repeat until the whole piece of fabric is covered with cirlces

Fabric 2: Diamonds

1. Concertina fold your fabric until it is all pleated, creating folds approximately 5–6 cm (2–2½ in) wide.
2. Fold your pleated fabric into triangles along the pleats.
3. On each corner clamp your triangular folds using wooden blocks secured with cable ties.
4. Now you are ready to dye your fabrics!
5. Place your fabrics in a tub of warm water with 1 teaspoon of detergent, massage. This will help the indigo dye to be absorbed evenly throughout the fabric. Squeeze out excess liquid.
6. Place in the vat for 2–5 minutes

depending on the depth of color you are after. You could pull out the fabric pieces at different times to create a contrast in color for each patch.

7. Remove and squeeze out any excess dye using an old towel.

Fabric 1: Cut the string and remove to reveal the design.

Fabric 2: Cut the cable ties, remove the wooden blocks and unfold to reveal your design.
  1. Watch the green color oxidize and turn blue.
  2. Wash in water with 1 tablespoon of salt to help fix the color.
  3. Rinse the fabric pieces until the water runs clear and then hang them out to dry.

TO MAKE THE CUSHION:
Finished Dimensions are 50 x 50 cm (19½ x 19½ in)
  1. Cut 2 strips of your shibori sample fabrics to 53 x 28 cm (21 x 11 in). Choose designs that are different in scale and color to help define the shibori designs.
  2. Stitch the strips together using 1.5 cm (½ in) seam allowance to form a piece of fabric that measures 53 x 53 cm (21 x 21 in).
  3. Press seams open.
  4. Cut your backing fabric to 53 x 53 cm (21 x 21 in), giving you a 1.5 cm (½ in) seam allowance.

5. Put your patched and plain panels right sides together and put a pin at approximately 10 cm (4 in) from each end of the side seam where the zipper is to go.
6. Stitch on one side, using a 1.5 cm (½ in) seam allowance.
7. Stitch the zipper opening with a regular width stitch until you get to your pins (at 10 cm/4 in) then change the longest width stitch so it is easy to remove after the zipper has gone in.
8. Open the seam and press flat.
9. Place the zipper down on the backside of the seam and pin.
10. Stitch the zipper into place at 1 cm (½ in) from the seam line.
11. Remove the stay stitch to open the side seam so you can open the zip.
12. Press flat.
13. Fold the two fabrics right sides together and sew the remaining 3 sides of the cushion with a seam allowance of 1.5 cm (½ in).
14. Open the zipper and pull through to the right side, pushing the corners out
15. Press and insert the cushion inner.

Note: You can create a really interesting and unique look by making lots of these cushions using all different fabrics.

Chevron Cushion Cover

This chevron design is very popular in home furnishings, so will be a great addition to your living room!

WHAT YOU WILL NEED:

- Sewing machine
- Thread
- Fabric for shibori — 55 x 55 cm (21½ x 21½ in) minimum
- Backing fabric (linen) 53 x 53 cm (21 x 21 in) (includes seam allowance)
- Zipper 30 cm (12 in)
- Cushion inner 50 x 50 cm (19½ x 19½ in)
- Tape measure
- Pins
- Scissors
- Wooden blocks x 8
- Cable ties
- Laundry pegs
- Dye vat (see page 13)
- Rubber gloves
- 2 x tubs of water, one with detergent (1 tablespoon to clean) and one with salt (1 tablespoon to fix the color)
- Drop sheet
- Drying rack

Notes: I have used linen for the front and back of the cushion and have created the same shibori design for both sides of the cushion.

You could make your cushion first and then dye it but it may shrink making the finished dimensions smaller than originally planned. You are also then restricted on how you can fold your cushion because of the zipper.

> Tip:
> Always cut the fabric bigger than the dimensions of the cushion inner, in case the fabric shrinks or frays when dyed.

SHIBORI TECHNIQUE:

1. First you must fold your fabric in a concertina fold approximately five times, which will make your fold about 8–9 cm (3–3½ in) wide.
2. Clamp your wooden blocks evenly across your folds at an angle. This will create a chevron design (zigzag effect).
3. Now it's ready to put in a tub of warm water with 1 teaspoon of detergent, massage. This will help the indigo dye to be absorbed evenly throughout the

fabric. Squeeze out excess liquid.

4. Place in the vat for 2–5 minutes, depending on the depth of color you are after.
5. Remove and squeeze out any excess dye using an old towel to absorb the excess.
6. Remove the clamps and wood blocks and unfold to reveal your design.
7. Watch the green color oxidize and turn blue.
8. Wash in water with 1 tablespoon of salt to help fix the color.
9. Rinse until the water runs clear and hang out to dry.

Peg clamp variation:

1. Fold your fabric into five folds using the concertina method. Then you will use laundry pegs either evenly on both sides or in groups of three as I have to clamp your folds and create a small resist dots along the fold. Do the same for the backing fabric.
2. Place your folded and clamped fabrics into the vat for 5–10 minutes, depending on the intensity of color you want.
3. Remove from the vat and squeeze out any excess dye into an old towel.
4. Remove the pegs and unfold the fabric. Rinse in water until the fabric no longer drips dye and hang on the clothes line to dry.

TO MAKE THE CUSHION:

1. Trim your Shibori fabric so it measures 53 x 53 cm (21 x 21 in) (this includes seam allowance)
2. Cut your backing fabric to 53 x 53 cm (21 x 21 in) (this includes seam allowance).
3. Put your front and back pieces of fabric right sides together. Put a pin at 10 cm (4 in) from each end of the side seam where the zipper is to go.
4. Stitch the side of your cushion with a regular width stitch until you get to your pins (at 10 cm/4 in) then change the longest width stitch (stay stitch) so it is easy to remove after the zipper has gone in.
5. Open the seam and press flat.
6. Place the zipper down on the backside of the seam and pin.
7. Stitch the zipper into place at 1 cm (½ in) from the seam line.
8. Remove the stay stitch to open the side seam so you can open the zip.
9. Press flat.
10. Fold the two fabrics right sides together and sew the remaining three sides of the cushion with a seam allowance of 1.5 cm (½ in).
11. Open the zipper and pull through to the right side, pushing the corners out.
12. Press and insert the cushion inner.

Embroidery Hoop Frames

A very simple and inexpensive way of filling those empty walls with original and interesting art you have created yourself!

YOU WILL NEED:

- White silk or cotton cut into squares
  1 square = 35 x 35 cm (14 x 14 in)
  1 square = 30 x 30 cm (12 x 12 in)
  1 square = 25 x 25 cm (9¾ x 9¾ in)
- Embroidery Hoops – 3 sizes: 20 cm (8 in), 25 cm (9¾ in), 30 cm (12 in)
- Scissors
- Chalk
- Removable picture hooks x 3
- 2 x Jar lids
- Clamps
- 4 x wood blocks (15 cm (6 in) long and various thickness)
- Cable ties
- Dye vat (see page 13)
- Rubber gloves
- Drop sheet
- Drying rack

SHIBORI TECHNIQUE:

Pick three different Shibori techniques to give the artwork some interest. Think about the scale and the placement of the design. I have picked a diagonal design, a large spot and a design that has both diagonals and spots to tie the designs together.

Fabric one

1. Fold your fabric in half, then fold each half again back on itself to create a concertina fold.
2. Fold your strip of folded fabric again using the concertina fold until the fabric is folded into a square.
3. Place one jar lid on one side and the other lid on the other side of the folded fabric. This will be clamped and will resist the dye when placed in the dye vat.

Fabric two and three

1. Fold your fabric using the concertina fold, making your pleats about 3 cm (1¼ in) wide. This will give you a smaller pattern when you clamp it, giving you an alternative scaled design to the first fabric.
2. When you clamp your folded fabric, try placing your wooden blocks on angles or in groups to create different patterns. Secure your wooden blocks with tightly fastened cable ties, which are around the blocks to resist the dye.

3. Place all your fabric into the dye vat at the same time but remove them at different times to give you a variation in the depth of color. This will also give you a more interesting design when you hang them on the wall as a group.

TO MAKE THE EMBROIDERY HOOPS:

1. When you have finished your shibori dyeing, decide which design works best with each size of embroidery hoop.
2. Once you have decided, place the larger of the hoops on the fabric, then mark a line on the outside of the hoop 1 cm (½ in) from the hoop edge. Use chalk, as it is easy to remove. Cut on the chalk line.
3. Keep your offcuts for another project. Place the fabric between the inner hoop and outer hoop and tighten the clamp to secure.
4. They are ready to hang on the wall. I used removable hooks on the wall.

Note: You could add to this group if you want to. Groups look better when you hang in odd numbers, so hang 3, 5, 7, etc.

Make-up Bag

A very handy bag that is easy to make and can be used for many things. You can make them in various sizes but I in this project I will give you the instructions for the small bag.

WHAT YOU WILL NEED:

- Shibori fabric — 30 x 112 cm (12 x 44 in) (preferably linen or heavy cotton to give the bag body)
- Zipper, at least 25 cm (10 in)
- Lining fabric that compliments your shibori
- Thread
- Interfacing (optional for stiffening of the bag)
- Scrap for the zipper end pull

FABRICATION:

I have used 100 per cent cotton fabric. I have concertina folded the fabric at approximately 5 cm (½ in) folds and then folded the fabric in a triangular fold, clamping with wooden blocks across the corners of the folded triangle. This will give you a diamond pattern.

CONSTRUCTION:

1. Cut 2 pieces of fabric at 26 x 18 cm (10 x 8 in) for outside and 2 pieces at 26 x 18 cm (10 x 8 in) for the lining. All seam allowances are 1.5 cm (½ in).
2. Optional: Cut iron-on interfacing to iron on the back of the outside fabric to stiffen.
3. Lay one exterior piece right side up, lay zipper (teeth side down) on top with the zipper pull at the left, aligning zipper tape edge to the raw edges of the top of the exterior piece.
4. Tuck in pull-side zipper end, just bend it 90 degrees. You may choose to sew it down, or just pin it in place like I did. Make sure the metal bit of the zipper is just about 2 cm (¾ in) away from the left edge.
5. Layer lining piece on top, right side down on top of zipper.
6. Pin and baste. You can skip this part but basting really does help things from slipping around too much.
7. Use your zipper foot and a 1.5 cm (½ in) seam allowance. Sew over basting stitches, but not all the way to the end.
8. At about 2.5 cm (1 in) before the edge of the fabric, stop, backstitch, and then pull the zipper away from the seam, bending it down out of the way, in towards the fabrics. The whole point is to pull it out of the way so it doesn't get caught in the seam. Continue stitching along the fabrics until the edge.

9. Flip so that the fabrics are wrong sides facing and press.

10. Lay the remaining exterior piece right side up. Lay the zipper (with fabrics attached) on to, teeth side down, with the zipper pull at the right. Tuck in the pull side zipper end, just bend it 90 degrees, like before, making sure the metal bit of the zipper is just over 2 cm (¾ in) away from the right edge.

11. Lay the lining piece right side down on top. Pin and baste.

12. Using the zipper foot and a 1.5 cm (½ in) seam allowance, sew over basting stitches, but not all the way to the end.

13. Again, about 2.5 cm (1 in) before the edge of the fabric, stop, backstitch, and then pull the zipper away from the seam, bending it down, in towards the fabrics.

14. Continue stitching along the fabrics until the edge. Flip so that the fabrics are wrong sides facing and press. DO NOT topstitch along either side of the zipper at this point (we'll be doing that in another step towards the end).

15. Flip so that the exterior fabrics are right sides together and the lining pieces are right sides together (with the zipper hidden in the middle).

16. Open the sipper at least halfway at this point.

17. Pin and sew around all edges, leaving approximately a 8 cm (3 in) opening in the bottom (or side) of the lining. You'll be using a 1.5 cm (½ in) seam allowance. Be sure to get close to the metal zipper ends on one side, and bending the zipper end down into the pouch on the other side making sure it doesn't get caught in the seam.

18. Box the corners by pinching each corner together and aligning each corresponding side/bottom seam, one corner at a time. Use a ruler and water-soluble marker to mark a line perpendicular to the side seam 6 cm (2½ in) long.

19. Sew along that line and trim the seam allowance. Do this for all four corners (two exterior, two lining).

20. Pull the pouch right side out through the opening you left in the lining. Tuck in raw edges of opening. Sew opening in lining closed using a small seam allowance by machine (sewing close to the fold as in the above picture) or hand stitch the opening closed. Push lining into exterior. Press around entire opening and carefully along the zipper.

21. Topstitch using a slightly longer stitch length (and taking your time) around the entire opening of the pouch.

22. Trim the zipper tail so that you have about 2.5 cm (1 in) of space past the pouch's side (be careful not to slide the zipper pull off the zipper!).

23. For making the zipper pull tab, take a 5 x 7.5 cm (2 x 3 in) piece of fabric.

24. Press all edges in by 1.5cm (½ in), slip over zipper end.

25. Fold in half, sew around all four edges of the tab.

Gift Cards

I have used leftover fabric for this project. A small piece of shibori cut into a circle gives you an original card showing the different shibori techniques.

WHAT YOU WILL NEED:
- Card
- Envelopes
- Shibori fabric
- Glue
- Thread
- Sewing machine
- Cutting blade
- Cutting board
- Steel ruler
- Set square

SHIBORI TECHNIQUE:
I have used sample fabrics or offcuts from other shibori projects for this project.

CONSTRUCTION:
1. Decide on the size of your card. I have found an envelope size I like, so will fold my cards to fit into the envelope.
2. Using a cutting blade and a steel ruler, cut out your card using a setsquare to ensure the card is square.
3. Find the middle of the card. Using a blunt edge knife, score your card to create a clean, crisp fold.
4. Cut your shibori fabric into the circle.
5. Centre your fabric on the card and glue into place.
6. Use your sewing machine to stitch your fabric onto the card, about 5 mm (¼ in) from the edge of the fabric.
7. To conceal the stitching on the back of the card, I have inserted and glued another card inside. This will give you a really neat finish and frames the design on the front of the card.
8. Create more cards using your shibori samples to make a beautiful collection of cards.

Lamp Shade

This is a great way of up-cycling a tired lampshade. I picked this lampshade up from charity shop and thought I would give it a new lease of life!

YOU WILL NEED:
- Lampshade (in a neutral cream or off-white color so as not to detract from the shibori fabric placed on top)
- Silk satin for your shibori (the amount will be determined by the size of your lampshade)
- Wood blocks x 6 (15 cm/6 in) long
- Cable ties
- Dye vat (see page 13)
- Rubber gloves
- 2 x tubs of water, one with detergent (1 tablespoon to clean) and one with salt (1 tablespoon to fix the color)
- Drop sheet
- Drying rack
- Hot glue gun
- Glue
- Scissors
- Tape measure
- Paper to trace pattern to cut fabric

SHIBORI TECHNIQUE:
I have used silk as my base cloth but you could use a cotton or linen. Make sure you check how the fabric looks on the lampshade against the light because some fabrics look better than others with a light behind them.

1. Firstly, measure the circumference of the widest part of your lampshade so you prepare enough fabric to cover the lampshade.
2. Cut your fabric, plus a little extra.
3. Concertina fold your fabric with folds of approximately 8–10 cm (3–4 in) pressing as you go with the iron.
4. Using wood blocks, clamp on an angle across the folded fabric and secure with cable ties.
5. Place the next wood blocks in the opposite angle, which will mirror the image.
6. Repeat this pattern across the folded fabric.
7. Now it's ready to put in a tub of warm water with1 teaspoon of detergent, massage. This will help the indigo dye to be absorbed evenly throughout the fabric.
8. Place in the vat for 2–5 minutes depending on the depth of color you are after.
9. Remove and squeeze out any excess dye using an old towel.
10. Cut the cable ties and remove the wood blocks. Unfold to reveal the design.
11. Watch the green color oxidize and turn blue.

12. Wash in water with 1 tablespoon of salt to help fix the color.
13. Rinse until the water runs clear, then hang out to dry.

TO MAKE THE LAMPSHADE:

1. Trace your lamp shape onto paper to make a pattern to cut from.
2. Lay out your fabric and place the pattern on top.
3. Cut the pattern out, adding 2 cm (¾ in) at the top and bottom so the fabric can be rolled over the frame and glued into place.
4. Start to glue at the seam line of the lampshade. Put a spot of glue at the top, then run a very fine line of hot glue down the seam line.
5. Place your printed fabric on the glue line. Be careful not to pull or stretch the fabric to maintain its shape.
6. Moving around the top and the bottom, add small amounts of glue.
7. When you get to the end of the gluing, fold over the end to create a neat edge to glue into place.
8. Now it's time to turn the top and bottom edges over and glue down, neatly tucking the fabric in around the frame.
9. Trim any loose threads and put your new lampshade on its base.

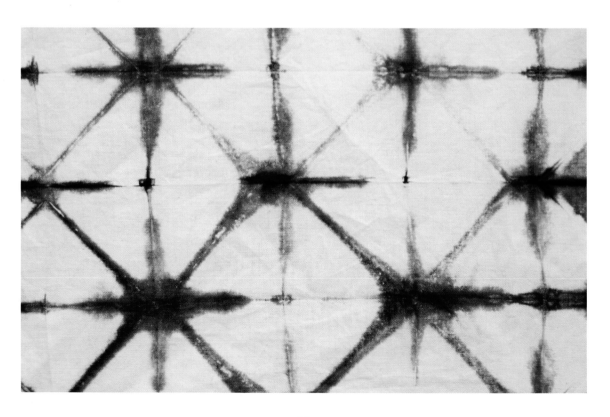

Napkins

This is a lovely project to do as a gift for someone and looks great if you coordinate with your table runner.

If you don't sew or you have some old plain white cotton napkins that are very tired, you could use those to shibori. You could also purchase plain white cotton or linen napkins to do this shibori technique.

YOU WILL NEED:

- Fabric — linen works well. (If your fabric is 120 cm/47 in wide, you will need 1.5 m/5 ft)
- Sewing machine
- Matching thread
- Scissors
- Square wooden blocks x 12
- Clamps x 6
- Dye vat (see page 13)
- Rubber gloves
- 2 x tubs of water, one with detergent (1 tablespoon to clean) and one with salt (1 tablespoon to fix the color)
- Drop sheet
- Drying rack

TO MAKE THE NAPKINS:

1. Cut your fabric into six pieces that are 47 x 45.5 cm (18½ x 18 in). (This includes seam allowance.)
2. Iron any creases out of your fabric.
3. Fold the edge 75 mm (¼ in) and press the hem.
4. Turn your fabric again 75 mm (¼ in) and topstitch the hem using thread that matches your fabric best.
5. Finish your stitching by reverse stitching to reinforce.
6. Clip any loose threads and press.

SHIBORI TECHNIQUE:

1. Concertina fold your napkin four times.
2. Fold your concertina fold in half and then again to create a square block of fabric. Press.
3. Place one of your square wooden blocks on one side of the fabric bundle and then place the second square block on the opposite side. Clamp to secure the wood blocks.
4. Your fabrics are now ready to put in a tub of warm water with 1 teaspoon of detergent. Massage. This will help the indigo dye to be absorbed evenly throughout the fabric.
5. Place in the vat for 2–5 minutes, depending on the depth of color you are after.
6. Remove and squeeze out any excess dye using an old towel to absorb the excess.
7. Cut the cable ties, remove the wood blocks and unfold to reveal the design.

8. Watch the green color oxidize and turn blue.
9. Wash in water with 1 tablespoon of salt to help fix the color.
10. Rinse the fabrics until the water runs clear and hang out to dry.

Variation:
I have done a bundle of six all using the same shibori technique but you could do all different shibori techniques to experiment, giving a unique set of napkins.

Woven Necklace

I used some of my daughter's old stained white cotton t-shirts for this project, rather than throwing them in the bin.

YOU WILL NEED:

- T-shirt fabric, approximately 1 m (3 ft)
- Tape measure
- Scissors
- Hot glue gun
- Dye vat
- Rubber gloves
- 2 x tubs of water, one with detergent (1 tablespoon to clean) and one with salt (1 tablespoon to fix the color)
- Drop sheet
- Drying rack

Note: You can do this project two ways and get different results:
1. Make your woven necklace up first and then use a shibori technique, such as rubber bands wrapped around it, to give a striped effect.
OR
2. Shibori your fabric first, then cut it up and make your woven necklace. This will give you a random pattern and you can also use a different intensity of color for each strip, giving you a totally different look.

TO MAKE THE WOVEN NECKLACE:

1. It is helpful when learning a knot to use at least two colors of rope or cord so you don't mix up where you are in the knot.

TIP:
The crown knot uses at least four strands of cord and makes a nice thick chain of knots called a sennet.

---

2. Cut four strips of fabric approximately 7 cm (2¾ in) wide (don't worry if your cut edge is shaggy it wont matter).
3. Stretch the strips so the cut edges curl.
4. Tie all four strips together at one end using a thin scrap of the same fabric approximately 30 cm (12 in) long. This will secure them all together and give you one end to tie your necklace on and the shorter end is wound around the four strips to give a tidy finish, as shown.
5. Cut off any bulky ends to keep it tidy.
6. Now it's time to weave.
7. To tie the crown knot, hold your four cords in a bunch.

8. Cross the first cord over the second cord.

9. Cross the second cord over the third cord.

10. Cross the third cord over the fourth cord.

11. Pull the fourth cord under the first cord.

12. Pull all of the cords tight and continue with the same four steps to create a chain of knots. It does not matter which cord you start with as long as you cross it over the one next to it in the same order every time.

13. When you have the desired length, bring all four strips together using a long single strip to tie them together as tightly as possible, leaving one long end which will become the tie for the necklace.

SHIBORI TECHNIQUE:

1. I have wrapped elastic bands around the necklace at various points of the woven section and offset them so they are not all the same spacing, for added interest, or use various thickness of elastic bands to give texture to your pattern.

2. Prepare your dye vat and place your necklace into the vat gently and leave it submerged for 2–3 minutes. If you want your color to be more intense, leave it in the vat for longer.

3. Remove and squeeze out any excess dye using an old towel to absorb the excess.

4. Cut the elastic bands to reveal your design.

5. Watch the green color oxidize and turn blue.

6. Wash in water with 1 tablespoon of salt to help fix the color.

7. Rinse until the water runs clear and then hang out to dry.

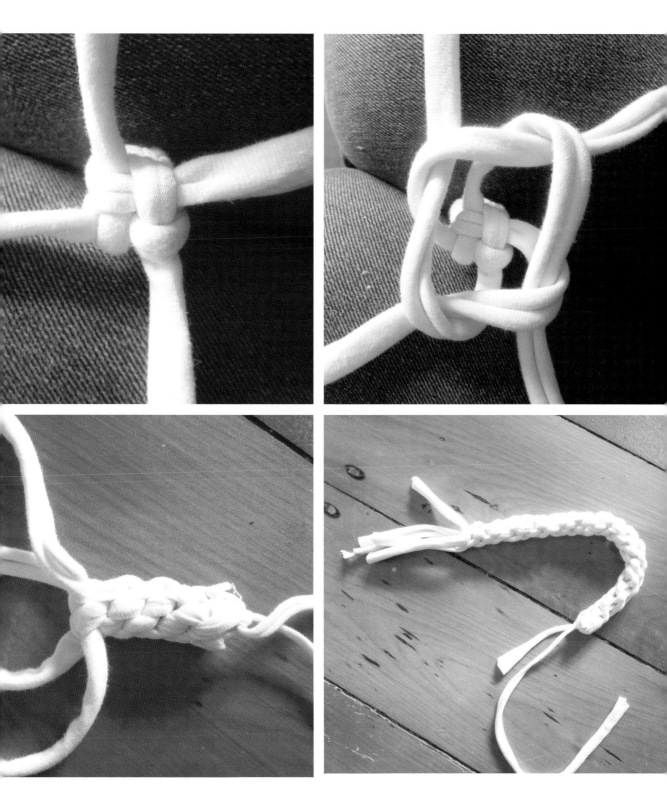

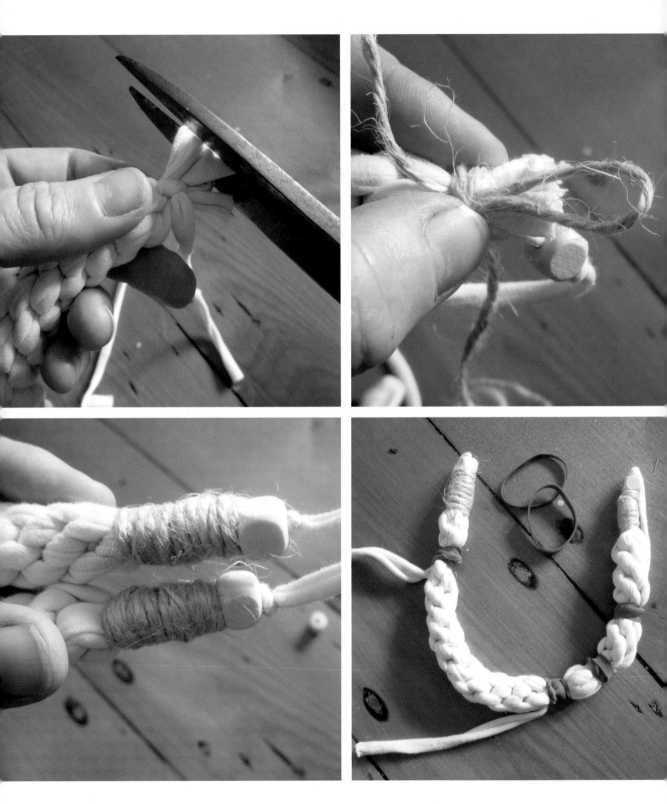

Pillow Shams

I have decided to do four pillow shams for my double bed so I can use all four at once or rotate two at a time. A really simply project and looks great in a beach house.

YOU WILL NEED:

- Plain white 100 per cent cotton pillow shams x 4
- Wood blocks
- Cable ties
- Clamps
- Dye vat (see page 13)
- Rubber gloves
- 2 x tubs of water, one with detergent (1 tablespoon to clean) and one with salt (1 tablespoon to fix the color)
- Drop sheet
- Drying rack

SHIBORI TECHNIQUE:

For this project, it is important to create designs that work well together, creating interest and variation in scale will help to achieve this.

Different scales of design can be achieved by using large or small concertina folds. The larger folds will give a larger scaled design whereas small tight folds will give a more intricate design.

Pillow sham 1:

1. Fold in half lengthways.
2. Fold one side in half again. Flip the pillow case and fold the other side in half. The sham should look like a long thin strip of fabric.
3. Start at the end that doesn't have the openings and fold into a triangle.
4. Flip your fabric over and fold another triangle.
5. Press with an iron.
6. Clamp through the middle of the triangle with two pieces of wood fastened tightly with cable ties.
7. Now it's ready to put in a tub of warm water with 1 teaspoon of detergent. Massage. This will help the indigo dye to be absorbed evenly throughout the fabric.
8. Place in the vat for 2–5 minutes depending on the depth of color you are after.
9. Remove and squeeze out any excess dye using an old towel to absorb the excess.
10. Cut the cable ties, remove the clamps and wood blocks and unfold to reveal your design.
11. Watch the green color oxidize and turn blue.
12. Wash in water with 1 tablespoon of salt to help fix the color.
13. Rinse until the water runs clear.
14. Hang on the line to dry.

Pillow Sham 2:

1. Fold in half lengthways.
2. Fold one side in half, then flip and do the same on the other side. This is called a concertina fold.
3. The fabric should look like a long strip. Fold in half and then fold again to create an oblong.
4. Clamp through the middle of the folded oblong and fasten tightly with cable ties.
5. Now it's ready to put in a tub of warm water with a teaspoon of detergent, massage. This will help the indigo dye to be absorbed evenly throughout the fabric.
6. Place in the vat for 2–5 minutes depending on the depth of color you are after.
7. Remove and squeeze out any excess dye using an old towel to absorb the excess.
8. Cut the cable ties, remove the clamps and wood blocks and unfold to reveal your design.
9. Watch the green color oxidize and turn blue.
10. Wash in water with 1 tablespoon of salt to help fix the color.
11. Rinse until the water runs clear and then hang out to dry.

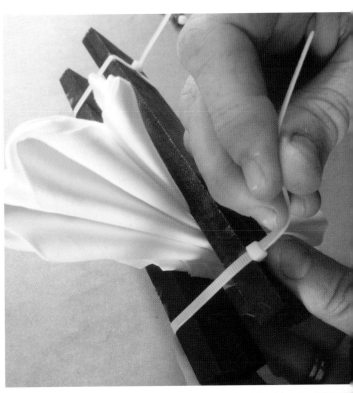

Pillow sham 1

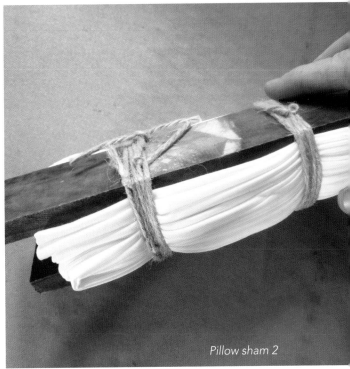

Pillow sham 2

Silk Scarf

I love shibori dyeing because you never quite know what you are going to get until you open the fabric up and hang it out to dry. The challenge with this technique is to try and create a design with some regularity in the pattern. To achieve a good pattern precise folding, ironing clamping or tying will make all the difference to your finished design.

I would cut and construct your scarf before dyeing it so you can engineer the shibori dye pattern and your stitched hem will be dyed the same color as the fabric.

YOU WILL NEED:

- Silk habitae (light weight silk) fabric 2 m (6½ ft) long (you will have leftover fabric to make more scarves)
- Sewing machine
- Thread
- Sewing needle
- Scissors
- Iron
- Dye vat (see page 13)
- Rubber gloves
- 2 x tubs of water, one with detergent (1 tablespoon to clean) and one with salt (1 tablespoon to fix the color)
- Drop sheet
- Drying rack

Note: I have cut one piece of 100 per cent silk habitae 30 cm (12 in) wide and the full length of the fabric, which is 182 cm (72 in). This will give you 1 cm (½ in) for hemming on all sides of your scarf.

TO MAKE THE SCARF:

1. Cut your fabric to 30 cm (12 in) wide x 182 cm (72 in) long, which includes your 1 cm (½ in) hem allowance on all sides.
2. Use your iron to turn all edges 5 cm (2 in) and turn again to form a hem.
3. Stitch all the way as close to the folded edge as possible. Finish with some back stitching to reinforce.
4. Press with an iron.

Optional: If your fabric is really lightweight you may want to add a trim or braid on each end to give it more weight. This should be done after you have completed your shibori.

SHIBORI TECHNIQUE:

1. Fold your scarf in half and then fold one side again and flip to fold the other side again.
2. Thread your needle with a contrast thread, making it long so you have plenty to stitch with.
3. Sandwiching all the layers together, stitch across your scarf at intervals using a running thread. When you get to the other side, cut your thread

leaving a long tail, which you will use to gather the thread when you have completed all the stitched lines.

4. Once you have completed your lines gather them up as tightly as you can. The gathering will resist the dye and give a watery pattern. Knot the thread to keep the gathering tight.

5. Now it is ready to put in a tub of warm water with 1 teaspoon of detergent, massage. This will help the indigo dye to be absorbed evenly throughout the fabric.

6. Place in the vat for 2–5 minutes,

depending on the depth of color you are after.

7. Remove and squeeze out any excess dye using an old towel to absorb the excess.

8. Cut the stitching, remove the gathers and unfold to reveal your design

9. Watch the green color oxidize and turn blue.

10. Wash in water with 1 tablespoon of salt to help fix the color.

11. Rinse until the water runs clear and hang out to dry.

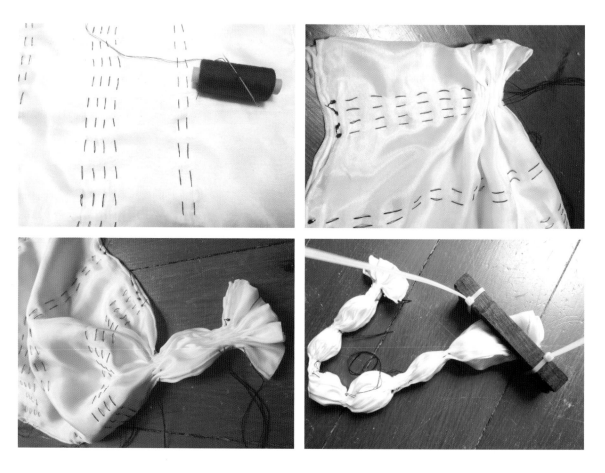

Girl's Skirt

This is a really easy skirt to make with no buttons or zippers and can be any length or fullness you want!

WHAT YOU WILL NEED:

- White linen or cotton fabric
- 3 cm (1¼ in) wide non-roll elastic (Length = waist measurement plus 2.5 cm/1 in)
- 2 safety pins
- Sewing machine
- Sewing thread
- Elastic bands
- Dye vat (see page 13)
- Rubber gloves
- 2 x tubs of water, one with detergent (1 tablespoon to clean) and one with salt (1 tablespoon to fix the color)
- Drop sheet
- Drying rack

PREPARE FABRIC FOR SHIBORI:

1. First measure the person's waist (my daughter's waist is 65 cm/25½ in) and double it for the gathering, totalling 130 cm (51 in). If your fabric isn't very wide you can cut two pieces half the total width and join them at each side making side seams of 1.5 cm (½ in) width.
2. Measure the waist to the knee (for the project shown it is 44 cm/ 17 in) adding 3.5 cm (1¼ in) for the waistband and 2.5 cm (1 in) for the hem. The total length for this project: 50 cm (19½ in). This length may vary if you want your skirt longer or shorter.
3. Cut a rectangle measuring 130 x 50 cm (51 x 19½ in) total. Now that you have the cut fabric for the skirt you can follow the steps for shibori technique.

SHIBORI TECHNIQUE:

1. Concertina fold the whole piece of fabric with small folds approx 3–4 cm (1¼ –1 ½ in) wide, pressing with the iron as you go.
2. Wrap with elastic bands at intervals along the pleated fabric, which will give you a striped design.
3. You can either space your elastic evenly or unevenly. I have decided to gradate my elastic for added interest.
4. Now it's ready to put in a tub of warm water with 1 teaspoon of detergent. Massage. This will help the indigo dye to be absorbed evenly throughout the fabric. Squeeze out excess liquid.
5. Place in the vat for 2–5 minutes, depending on the depth of color you are after.
6. Remove and squeeze out any excess dye using an old towel to absorb the excess.

7. Cut the elastic bands and remove. Unfold to reveal your design.
8. Watch the green color oxidize and turn blue.
9. Wash in water with 1 tablespoon of salt to help fix the color.
10. Rinse until the water runs clear and hang out to dry.

TO MAKE THE SKIRT:

1. Cut your elastic to the same measurements as the waist plus 2.5 cm (1 in) to overlap.
2. Fold over your fabric with right sides together to match up the side seams.
3. Sew down the side using a 1.5 cm (½ in) seam allowance.
4. Iron the seam open.
5. To create the casing for the elastic, turn your fabric right side out and turn raw edge 1 cm (½ in) and press.
6. Fold the same edge 3.5 cm (1¼ in) in, creating the casing for the elastic.
7. Stitch 5 mm (¼ in) from the folded edge all the way around, leaving 10 cm (4 in) at the end as an opening to thread your elastic through the casing.
8. Attach a safety pin to one end of the elastic and start threading it by inserting through the opening, pushing the safety pin through. Before you go too far, pin the other end of the elastic near to the opening so you don't put the elastic all the way through.
9. Pull all the way through and remove the safety pins, (making sure that you have not twisted the elastic) overlap the ends to about 2.5 cm (1 in), stitching back and forwards a few times to give a really strong join.
10. Pull the elastic so it is evenly gathered around the entire skirt.
11. Stitch the casing opening closed, making sure you back stitch at the beginning and end to reinforce.
12. Prepare the hem line by turning and pressing the raw edge 5 mm (¼ in).
13. Turn the edge again depending on the skirt length. You can play with the finished hem. I have chosen to turn it 1 cm (½ in), press, stitch.

TIP:
If you want to add some more detail you could apply bias binding or trim to the hem.

T-shirt

This is a really easy project to do. My kids had a go with some plain white t-shirts that I bought. You could also use an old, tired white t-shirt to give it a new look.

YOU WILL NEED:
- White cotton t-shirt (cotton/elastin t-shirt will also work well for shibori)
- Clamps
- Wooden blocks
- Cable ties
- Dye vat (see page 13)
- Rubber gloves
- 2 x tubs of water, one with detergent (1 tablespoon to clean) and one with salt (1 tablespoon to fix the color)
- Drop sheet
- Drying rack

SHIBORI TECHNIQUE:
For this project I found the easiest method is to fold and clamp the t-shirt because it is not a regular shape.

1. Find the middle of the t-shirt and fold into a concertina fold.
2. Clamp with wooden blocks at intervals across the t-shirt. I like to use three clamps and place two on half of the t-shirt and then offset the pattern with one on the other side of the center front.
3. Secure the blocks with cable ties.
4. Put prepared t-shirt into warm water that has 1 teaspoon of detergent in it to remove any stiffening agents, which are often put onto the garment to give a crisp finish for shop display. If it is an old t-shirt you will only need to wet it.
5. Make sure the fabric is saturated, then remove and squeeze excess water out of the fabric.
6. Put into your dye vat for 3–5 minutes or longer if you want a more intense deep color.
7. Remove from the vat and squeeze out the excess dye.
8. Remove clamps and unfold your fabric.
9. Let it oxidize (change from green to blue).
10. Rinse in cold water with 1 tablespoon of salt to help fix the color.
11. Hang on the clothes line to dry.

Tablecloth

The dimensions for this tablecloth are 145 x 250 cm (57 x 98 in). If your table is larger I would suggest using cotton sheeting, which will be wider.

YOU WILL NEED:

- White linen or heavy cotton canvas/sheeting (measure your table to get the correct dimensions adding 1.5 cm (½ in) for hemmed edge)
- Sewing machine
- White thread
- Wood blocks approximately 30 cm (in) long x 2.5 cm (in) wide
- Cable ties
- Clamps
- Dye vat (see page 13)
- Rubber gloves
- 2 x tubs of water, one with detergent (1 tablespoon to clean) and one with salt (1 tablespoon to fix the color)
- Drop sheet
- Drying rack

Note: Make your tablecloth before you do the shibori so that the hemming stitches are dyed the same color as the fabric.

TO MAKE THE TABLECLOTH:

1. Cut your fabric to 147 x 253 cm (58 x 100 in). Tthis includes 1.5 cm (½ in) for hem allowance.
2. Iron any creases out of your fabric.
3. Fold the edge in 75 mm (¼ in). Press.
4. Turn your fabric again 75 mm (¼ in) and topstitch the hem using white thread.
5. Finish your stitching by reverse stitching to reinforce.
6. Clip any loose threads and then iron.

SHIBORI TECHNIQUE:

To create an effective shibori design for large pieces of fabric, it is best to keep the design very simple. For this project I wanted the tablecloth to be predominantly blue as it won't show stains as much as a white cloth.

1. Fold your cloth in a concertina fold across the entire piece of fabric.
2. Fold the pleated fabric to form a triangle and then press with the iron.
3. Clamp with two pieces of wood (30 cm (12 in) long x 2.5 cm (1 in) wide) and hold in place using cable ties at each end as tightly as possible across the triangle.
4. Put the prepared fabric into warm water with 1 teaspoon of detergent.
5. Make sure the fabric is saturated. Remove, squeeze out excess water.
6. Put into your dye vat for 3–5 minutes or longer if you want a more intense deep color.

7. Remove from the vat and squeeze out excess dye.
8. Remove clamps and unfold your fabric.
9. Let it oxidize (change from green to blue).
10. Rinse in cold water with 1 tablespoon of salt to help fix the color.
11. Hang on the clothes line to dry.

Table Runner

Table runners are a quick and easy way to add color and style to a table. This Shibori table runner will give you a unique creative addition to your table setting.

YOU WILL NEED:

- White linen or heavy cotton canvas (finished dimensions will be 45 x 150 cm (18 x 59 in). This will vary depending on the length of your table so measure the length of the table and add 5 cm (2 in) to that measurement for seam allowances).
- Sewing machine
- Thread
- Triangular wooden blocks x 2
- Clamps x 2
- Iron
- Dye vat (see page 13)
- Rubber gloves
- 2 x tubs of water, one with detergent (1 tablespoon to clean) and one with salt (1 tablespoon to fix the color)
- Drop sheet
- Drying rack

TO MAKE THE TABLE RUNNER:

1. Cut the fabric to 50 x 155 cm (20 x 61 in) (or your table length plus 5 cm/ 2 in). This gives you a seam allowance of 2.5 cm (1 in) on each edge.
2. Fold your edge 12.5 mm (½ in) and press with an iron, turn again 12.5 mm (½ in) and stitch using your sewing machine. Make sure your corners are neatly turned and pressed before sewing.
3. Finish each side with a couple of reverse stiches to reinforce.
4. Now your table runner is ready for your shibori design before dyeing in the vat. I have chosen to use the Itajime technique for my design.

SHIBORI TECHNIQUE:

1. Fold your runner in half to mark the middle of the runner.
2. Make your first fold at one end of the runner approximately 70 cm (28 in) and then fold the opposite way until you have folded evenly the entire length of the runner making a concertina fold.
3. Fold the bundle in half and clamp with a triangle shape on each side of the bundle making sure they are opposite each other to create the same resist design on both sides. Clamp to hold in place.
4. Place your clamped fabric into warm water that has 1 teaspoon of kitchen detergent in it. This will make sure there is nothing in the fabric like stiffeners that may prevent the dye from penetrating the fabric.
5. Remove from the bucket and squeeze

out any excess water so as not to dilute the dye vat.

6. Place the clamped fabric into the dye vat for 5–10 minutes depending on how intense you want your color to be.
7. While your fabric is submerged, massage the folds with your fingers to help the dye to be absorbed.
8. Remove from the vat and squeeze excess dye from the fabric using an old towel.
9. Remove the clamps and resist shapes and unfold your fabric.
10. Watch the indigo change from green to blue because of oxidization.
11. Rinse in cold water to remove any excess dye then hang on the clothes line.

Atelrnative design idea

Dish Towel

This is a great way of testing the technique of Shibori. You can use a plain white linen dish towel and turn it into something special and original. This would make a lovely house warming gift. Enjoy!

YOU WILL NEED:
- A white linen dish towel
- Clamps/cable ties
- Jar lids x 2
- Dye vat (see page 13)
- Rubber gloves
- 2 x tubs of water, one with detergent (1 tablespoon to clean) and one with salt (1 tablespoon to fix the color)
- Drop sheet
- Drying rack

SHIBORI TECHNIQUE:
1. Fold the dish towel in half lengthways.
2. Fold in half again and flip it to fold the other side the same, making a concertina fold.
3. Fold the long strip in half and half again, flip and do the same with the other side.
4. Place your jar lid in the center of the bundle, turn over and place the second lid in the same position
5. Clamp with large clamps, depending on the strength of the clamp you may need two to hold into place.
6. Now it is ready to put in a tub of warm water with 1 teaspoon of detergent. Massage. This will help the indigo dye absorb evenly throughout the fabric.
7. Make sure the fabric is saturated and then remove and squeeze excess water out of fabric.
8. Place in the vat for 2–5 minutes, depending on the depth of color you are after.
9. Remove and squeeze out any excess dye using an old towel.
10. Remove the clamps and jar lids and unfold to reveal your design.
11. Watch the green color oxidize and turn blue.
12. Wash in water with 1 tablespoon of salt to help fix the color.
13. Rinse until the water runs clear, then hang out to dry.

> TIP:
> Iron the dish towel before it is totally dry to remove any creases.

Tote Bag

No more plastic bags for your shopping, you can make this bag using any fabric. This little project is a great gift and the size can be changed depending on your use.

YOU WILL NEED:
- White linen or heavy cotton canvas
- Lining fabric (which could be anything to compliment your shibori fabric)
- Heavy iron-on interfacing
- Canvas strapping (1 m/3 ft)
- Scissors
- Sewing machine
- Thread
- Pegs x 15
- Wooden blocks
- Cables ties
- Clamps
- Iron
- Dye vat (see page 13)
- Rubber gloves
- 2 x tubs of water, one with detergent (1 tablespoon to clean) and one with salt (1 tablespoon to fix the color)
- Drop sheet
- Drying rack

PREPARE FABRIC FOR SHIBORI
1. Cut your inner and outer fabric.
2. Cut two 45 x 35 cm (18 x 14 in) outer shibori fabrics.
3. Cut two 45 x 35 cm (18 x 14 in) inner lining fabric.
4. Cut two 45 x 35 cm (18 x 14 in) interfacing.
5. Cut two 50 cm (20 in) long canvas straps.
6. Using the inner and outer fabric pieces and the canvas strap, follow the shibori technique steps below.
7. Set aside the interfacing pieces for when you sew up the tote bag.

SHIBORI TECHNIQUE:
1. Fold one piece of the cut fabric in a concertina fold, approximately seven folds with a width of 4–5 cm (1½–2 in). Place clothes pegs on both sides of the folds to hold pleats, creating a spot resist design when dyed.
2. Fold the second piece in half and half again to create a concertina. Then fold from one end into a triangle folding across the concertina folds. Clamp with two square blocks diagonally across the triangle.
3. For the other two pieces, fold the same way. Fold in half and half again. Fold your long tube in half and half again to create a folded square. Use four wood blocks to clamp across the square. My wood blocks are slightly different sizes to create different width strips.
4. Secure the wooden blocks with cable ties.

5. Now they are ready to put in a tub of warm water with 1 teaspoon of detergent. Massage. This will help the indigo dye to be absorbed evenly throughout the fabric. Squeeze out excess liquid.

6. Place in the vat for 2–5 minutes depending on the depth of color you are after. You could pull out two of the four pieces at different times to create a contrast in color for your bag.

7. Remove and squeeze out any excess dye using an old towel.

8. Cut the cable ties and remove clamps. Unfold to reveal your design.

9. Watch the green color oxidize and turn blue.

10. Wash in water with 1 tablespoon of salt to help fix the color.

11. Rinse the fabric pieces until the water runs clear and then hang them out to dry.

12. Now you are ready to construct your bag.

TO MAKE UP THE BAG:

1. Iron your interfacing to the wrong side of the outer Shibori fabric rectangles. Make sure your iron is not too hot, just hot enough to activate the glue so it sticks to the fabric.

2. At the bottom edge of all your rectangles (outer and lining) cut out a small square of 5 x 5 cm (2 x 2 in) — this will form the base of the tote bag when it is sewn. (As shown in photo).

3. Pin the outer fabrics right side together and sew a straight 12.5 mm (½ in) seam along the sides and bottom of the piece. Leave the top and the two lower square corners unsewn.

4. Press seams open.

5. To create the gusset at the bottom of the bag, pinch your corners together, align the lower edge of the side seam and bottom seams in the center. (As shown in photo).

6. Pin the two seams (side and bottom) together and sew straight across the edge using a seam allowance of 12.5 mm (½ in). This will give depth to the bottom of the bag and create a flat bottom so your bag stands up.

7. Following the instructions above, sew the lining sides, bottom and corners.

8. Piece together the outer and inner bags by flipping the liner right side out and place inside the outer fabric so that the right sides are together.

9. Tuck the canvas straps between the inner and outer fabrics so that two edges of one strap face the front and the other two edges face the back of the bag. Pin the straps into place approximately 10 cm (4 in) from the side seams.

10. Pin the fabric edges together around the top perimeter of the bag opening.

11. Sew your bag opening by starting at one of the side seams and stitch a 12.5 mm (½ in) seam almost all the way around leaving an opening of about 10 cm (4 in) so you can turn the bag to the right side.

12. Pull both fabrics and straps though the opening. Press.
13. Topstitch around the top of the bag, which will reinforce the canvas straps and also close the opening.

14. Time to go shopping with your new bag!

Towels

This is a really lovely gift for someone or to freshen up your bathroom using bold designs to make a statement. Towels are bulky so it is important to keep the folding simple.

YOU WILL NEED:

- White 100 per cent cotton towel
- Wooden block shapes (round, square or triangular)
- Large clamps
- Dye vat (see page 13)
- Rubber gloves
- 2 x tubs of water, one with detergent (1 tablespoon to clean) and one with salt (1 tablespoon to fix the color)
- Drop sheet
- Drying rack

SHIBORI TECHNIQUE:

Towel 1:

1. Fold your towel in a concertina fold across the towel at approximately 15–20 cm (6–8 in) width folds.
2. Place your wood block across your folds on both sides and secure with cable ties. Prepare your cable ties on each end of the wood to prevent the wood from moving around causing the clamp to be unaligned. Repeat to create a stripe pattern.
3. Place your next blocks on an angle, which will give you a zigzag pattern.
4. Offset your wood clamps to create an asymmetrical design.

TIP:
Place your towel on the floor and press the wooden blocks down to get a really good compression on the towel which is being clamped to prevent dye from being absorbed, therefore giving a definite pattern.

Towel 2:

1. Fold your towel in a concertina fold horizontally at approximately 15–20 cm (6–8 in) width folds.
2. Fold the long strip in half (this will give you a mirror image on each side of the towel when you clamp your design.)
3. I used an oblong piece of wood which I then clamped with large clamps on each side of the wooden shape. Now the towels are ready for dyeing.
4. Place the towels in a tub of warm water with 1 teaspoon of detergent. Massage. This will help the indigo dye absorb evenly throughout the fabric and will remove any stiffeners that may be in the new towel.
5. Place in the vat for 2–5 minutes depending on the depth of color you are after.

Note: I found that you will need to keep the towel in the vat for 10 minutes to get a more vibrate intense color, otherwise you will get a faded denim look.

6. Remove and squeeze out any excess dye using an old towel to absorb the excess.
7. Cut the cable ties, remove the wood blocks and unfold.

8. Watch the green color oxidize and turn blue.
9. Wash in water with 1 tablespoon of salt to help fix the color.
10. Rinse the towels until the water runs clear and then hang out to dry.

The Up-Cycled Ottoman

This is a lovely idea to use both old jeans and shibori samples to create an up-cycled, practical and color co-ordinated piece of home furnishing.

YOU WILL NEED:

- Heavy white cotton fabric or canvas as it is durable
- 2 pairs of old denim jeans (maybe 3 pairs if they are skinny jeans)
- Bean bag stuffing x 3 bags
- 2 safety pins
- Sewing machine
- Sewing Thread
- Wooden block shapes – round, square or triangular, marble, dog clips
- Large Clamps
- Dye vat (see page 13)
- Rubber gloves
- 2 x tubs of water, one with detergent (1 tablespoon to clean) and one with salt (1 tablespoon to fix the color)
- Drop sheet
- Drying rack

SHIBORI TECHNIQUES:

1. Cut four panels with dimensions of 40 x 58 cm (15½ x 23 in). These will be your side panels for the ottoman. *Note: You could cut them slightly larger to do the shibori and then when they are ready to construct trim them to the correct measurements. This measurement includes a seam allowance of 1.5cm

2. Panel 1: Using marbles, divide your fabric up into sections by folding and marking the corners. Place a marble at each point, marked and wrap with an elastic band as tightly as possible. Alternatively, you can place your marbles randomly on the fabric giving a scattered rather than ordered pattern.

3. Panel 2: Fold in half lengthways, then concertina fold your fabric giving you four folded edges. Now fold triangles across the folded tube. Clamp the triangle at each corner with dog clips.

4. Panel 3: Fold your fabric in half to find the middle, then fold a concertina fold across the panel, then fold in half again. Clamp in the middle of the fabric with two wooden blocks secured with clamps.

5. Panel 4: Concertina fold across the panel at 8–10 cm (3–4 in) wide folds. Once you have finished folding, press with an iron and clamp on both sides of your folded fabric with bulldog clips.

6. Now your fabric panels are ready to put in a tub of warm water with 1 teaspoon of detergent, massage. This will help the indigo dye to be absorbed evenly throughout the fabric.

7. Place in the vat for 2–5 minutes depending on the depth of color you are after.
8. Remove and squeeze out any excess dye using an old towel to absorb the excess.
9. Cut the cable ties, elastics, remove the wood blocks, marbles and unfold to reveal your design.
10. Watch the green color oxidize and turn blue.
11. Wash in water with 1 tablespoon of salt to help fix the color.
12. Rinse the fabrics until the water runs clear and hang out to dry.

TO MAKE UP THE OTTOMAN:

1. Firstly, to make your denim squares unpick the leg seams of your jeans that don't have the top stitching detail and stitch both legs together. The topstitched detail will be in the center of each leg of the jeans as a detail. This should give you enough fabric to cut your 58 cm (23 in) squares from. If not, add more denim to get the required area.
2. Cut out two squares of your denim to 58 x 58 cm (23 x 23 in).
3. Cut your four sample shibori pieces to 40 x 58 cm (15½ x 23 in).
4. Sew the four shibori sample rectangles together, right sides facing to form the sides of the ottoman. Using 1.5 cm (½ in) seam allowance, start 1.5 cm (½ in) from the top, sew together stopping 1.5 cm (½ in) from the

bottom. Make sure you backstitch.
5. Sew your denim square to the top of the ottoman, aligning corners and sewing one side at a time. Using a 1.5 cm (½ in) seam allowance, raise the presser foot and pivot at each corner.
6. Sew the other denim square to the bottom of the ottoman, leaving a 10 cm (4 in) opening on one side for turning through and stuffing.
7. Stuff to the desired firmness and hand stitch the opening closed. I suggest doing this in a bathtub to keep the filling contained.

These are great in a kids' play area — cheap, sturdy and fun to make!

Wall Hanging

I have very high ceilings in my home, making it difficult to hang art that doesn't cost a fortune. This project is the perfect size to fill a space in my stairwell that is in need of a little focal creative wall hanging and the best thing is, this original piece of art won't break the bank!

YOU WILL NEED:

- Silk satin fabric 1.5 m (5 ft) in length – cut so your fabric is 47 x 1.5 cm (18½ x ½ in). This will give you 1 cm (½ in) for all seams
- Sewing thread
- Sewing machine
- Wooden dowel sticks x 2 (12 mm/½ in thick x 50 cm/19½ in long)
- String or fishing line to hang your wall hanging
- Wood blocks, approximately 30 cm (12 in) long x 2.5 cm (1 in) wide
- Cable ties
- Dye vat (see page 13)
- Rubber gloves
- 2 x tubs of water, one with detergent (1 tablespoon to clean) and one with salt (1 tablespoon to fix the color)
- Drop sheet
- Drying rack

Note: I would recommend doing the shibori before you construct the wall hanging so you can choose the correct size and orientation of the hanging, depending on the detail of your finished design.

SHIBORI TECHNIQUE:

1. Concertina fold your fabric down the length of the fabric with pleats approximately 8–10 cm (3–4 in) wide.
2. Fold your long strip of concertina-pleated fabric into triangles until half your fabric is folded.
3. Clamp the triangular section with wooden blocks on a diagonal. Secure with cable ties.
4. For the remainder of the folded fabric, place your other two wooden blocks on either side of the pleated fabric and position them on a diagonal.
5. Secure the wooden blocks with cable ties at each end.
6. Now they are ready to put in a tub of warm water with 1 teaspoon of detergent. Massage. This will help the indigo dye to be absorbed evenly throughout the fabric. Squeeze out excess liquid.
7. Place in the vat for 2–5 minutes, depending on the depth of color you are after.
8. Remove and squeeze out any excess dye using an old towel.
9. Remove the wooden blocks and unfold

to reveal your design.

10. Watch the green color oxidize and turn blue.

11. Wash in water with 1 tablespoon of salt to help fix the color.

12. Rinse the fabrics until the water runs clear and hang out to dry.

TO MAKE THE WALL HANGING:

1. Press the whole piece of fabric and then decide which end is going to be your top and bottom of the hanger.

2. Turn and press all edges 5 mm (¼ in).

3. Turn your side seams again 5 mm (¼ in) and stitch from top to bottom on both sides, close to the folded edge using a medium length stitch. Press.

4. Turn your top and bottom edge 5 mm (¼ in) and fold again to create a casing for the wooden dowel to be threaded through. The width of the casing will depend on the width of your dowel.

5. Stitch close to the folded edge to create the casing. Don't forget to back stitch at the beginning and end.

6. Thread your dowel through the top and bottom of your wall hanging.

7. You can tie a string or fishing line to the top dowel to hang your wall hanging.

Note: fishing line will not be so visible when used to hang your wall hanging.

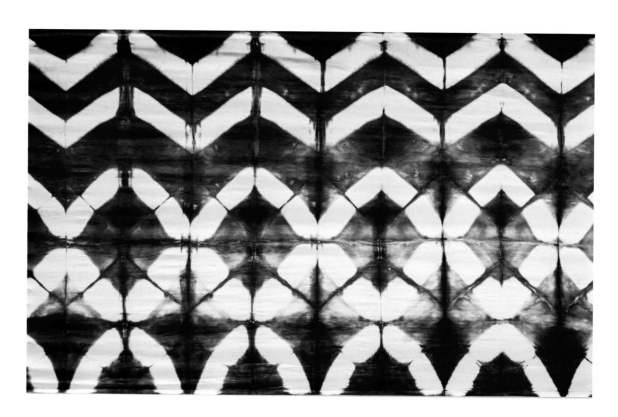

Oblong Cushion

This project is great for using up all those leftover pieces of shibori dyed fabrics. The finished cushion cover dimensions are 40 x 60 cm (16 x 24 in) so you will need to buy a cushion insert with the same dimensions.

YOU WILL NEED:

- Fabric Shibori and plain 100 per cent Cotton 120 cm (47 in)
- Zipper 40 cm (16 in)
- Sewing machine
- Thread
- Tape measure
- Scissors
- Cushion inner — 50 x 50 cm (20 x 20 in)
- Pins

SHIBORI TECHNIQUE:

To make the print:

1. The smallest panel is created by using rubber bands to wrap around pinched sections of fabric. Alternate the circles big and small by using more rubber bands for the large circles and less for the smaller.
2. For the thinner panel, concertina folded the fabric at approximately 8 cm (3 in) folds and then folded the fabric in a concertina fold again creating an oblong shape. Place a wooden block down the middle of the folded fabric and clamp with large clamps
3. Fold your fabric into a small concertina pleat approximately 3 cm (1 in) wide folds. Then wrap rubber bands at intervals along the folded fabric to create a resist.
4. When placing your prepared fabric into the vat, pull them out at different times so you get a variation in the color, which will add interest and a complexity to the finished cushion.

Construction:

1. Cut one panel of (A) Shibori fabric to 13 x 43cm (5 x 17 in)
2. Cut one panel (B) at 23 x 43 cm (9 x 17 in)
3. Cut one panel (C) at 33 x 43 cm (13 x 17 in). All panels includes your seam allowances of 1.5 cm (0.6 in)
4. Cut your backing piece 43 x 63 cm (17 x 25 in). This can either be a plain fabric or another contrasting piece of shibori.
5. Put your shibori panel's right sides together and stitch to join using a 1.5 cm (0.6 in) seam allowance.
6. Open and press the seams flat
7. Put the front and back pieces of fabric right sides together, and place a pin at 10 cm (4 in) from each end of the side seam where the zipper is to go.

8. Stitch the bottom edge of your cushion with a regular width stitch until you get to your pins (at 10 cm/4 in) then change the longest width stitch so it easy to remove after the zipper has gone in.

9. Open the seam and press flat.

10. Place the zipper down on the backside of the seam and pin.

11. Stitch the zipper into place at 1 cm (½ in) from the seam line

12. Remove the stay stitch to open the side seam so you can open the zip.

13. Press flat.

14. Fold the two pieces right sides together and sew the remaining three sides of the cushion with a seam allowance of 1.5 cm (½ in).

15. Open the zipper and pull through to the right side, pushing the corners out

16. Press and insert the 40 x 60 cm (16 x 24 in) cushion insert.

About the Author

Fiona Fagan grew up on a farm where she was exposed to the harsh beauty of outdoor landscapes.

Fiona trained firstly as a pattern maker and then as a Textile Designer, gaining a Bachelor of Design in Textile and Fashion Design. With over 25 years' experience in the fashion and textile industry, Fiona has designed fashion, bed linen, swimwear, children's wear, ceramic/homewares, soft furnishings, stationery and bath/body products.

Her designs draw inspiration from the land in which she was raised, with its contrasts, raw beauty and sensitivities. Inspired by the environment around her, Fiona's color palettes are often earthy with a strong infusion of vivid color.

Fiona is author of *Simply This*, a craft book that covers 30 projects, as well as being a breast cancer survivor, competitive dragon boater, outrigger, garden design enthusiast and mother of two beautiful girls!

For more on Shibori, follow Fiona on Instagram at www.instagram.com/simplythistextiles

Acknowledgments

I would like to thank my husband Mark and daughters Ella and Tessa for being supportive and patient while I wrote this book. I would like to thank Diane Ward at New Holland Publishers for giving me the opportunity to do this book. Thanks to my lecturer, Peter Van Sommer, for introducing me to Shibori while at University. Thank you to Sue Stubbs for her amazing aesthetic when it comes to photographing my projects. It has been wonderfully inspiring doing workshops to share my passion for Shibori with others who have given inspiration. Creativity is food for the soul, so I hope you enjoy this book and create lots of wonderful things.

First published in 2016 by New Holland Publishers Pty Ltd
London • Sydney • Auckland

The Chandlery Unit 704 50 Westminster Bridge Road London SE1 7QY United Kingdom
1/66 Gibbes Street Chatswood NSW 2067 Australia
5/39 Woodside Ave Northcote, Auckland 0627 New Zealand

www.newhollandpublishers.com

A record of this book is held at the British Library and the National Library of Australia.

ISBN 9781742578491

Managing Director: Fiona Schultz
Publisher: Diane Ward
Project Editors: Holly Willsher, Jessica McNamara
Designer: Lorena Susak
Production Director: James Mills-Hicks
Printer: Times International Printing, Malaysia

10 9 8 7 6 5 4 3 2 1

Keep up with New Holland Publishers on Facebook
www.facebook.com/NewHollandPublishers